W9-BYY-083

Growing Readers

New Hanover County Public Library

Purchased with
New Hanover County Partnership for Children
and Smart Start Funds

MEATS AND PROTEINS

by Robin Nelson

New Hanover County Public Library
201 Chestnut Street
Wilmington, NC 28401

Lerner Publications Company · Minneapolis

We need to eat many kinds
of food to be healthy.

We need to eat foods in the
meat and **protein** group.

We can eat meat, **poultry**,
fish, beans, eggs, and nuts.

Amount/Serving	%DV*	Amount/Serving	%DV*
Total Fat 16g	**25%**	**Total Carb.** 7g	**2%**
Sat. Fat 3g	**16%**	Dietary Fiber 2g	**9%**
Cholest. 0mg	**0%**	Sugars 3g	
Sodium 150mg	**6%**	**Protein** 8g	

Iron 4% • Riboflavin 2% • Niacin 20% • Vitamin E 10%
Not a significant source of vitamin A. vitamin C, and calcium.

These foods give us protein and **fat**.

Protein helps build our
bodies.

Fat gives us energy and keeps our bodies warm.

We need two **servings** of
meat and protein each day.

We can eat a hamburger.

We can eat fish.

We can eat turkey.

We can eat shrimp.

We can eat beans.

We can eat eggs.

We can eat peanut butter.

We can eat nuts.

Meat and protein foods
keep me healthy.

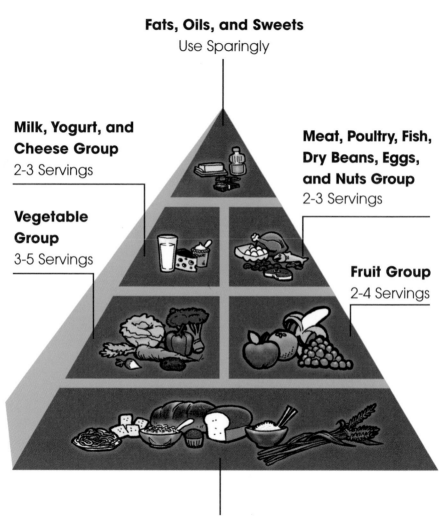

Fats, Oils, and Sweets
Use Sparingly

Milk, Yogurt, and Cheese Group
2-3 Servings

Meat, Poultry, Fish, Dry Beans, Eggs, and Nuts Group
2-3 Servings

Vegetable Group
3-5 Servings

Fruit Group
2-4 Servings

Bread, Cereal, Rice, and Pasta Group
6-11 Servings

Meat, Poultry, Fish, Dry Beans, Eggs, and Nuts Group

The food pyramid shows us how many servings of different foods we should eat every day. The meat, poultry, fish, dry beans, eggs, and nuts group is on the third level of the food pyramid. You need 2–3 servings from this group every day. The foods in the meat, poultry, fish, dry beans, eggs, and nuts group are good for you because they have protein. Protein helps our bodies grow.

Meat and Protein Facts

 The average child will eat 1,500 peanut butter sandwiches before graduating from high school.

 The peanut is not a nut. It is a legume and belongs to the pea family.

 November is National Peanut Butter Lover's Month.

 Hens lay one egg every 24 to 26 hours.

Beef comes from cattle and gives our bodies iron, zinc, protein, and B-vitamins. These nutrients are an important part of a healthy diet.

 Pork is meat we get from pigs. Pigs give us pork chops, ham, bacon, spareribs, sausage, and pork roasts.

Glossary

 fat – parts of food that give you energy

 meat – parts of animals we eat

 poultry – meat from birds like chickens, turkeys, ducks, and geese

 protein – parts of food that give us energy and help build bones, hair, muscles, and skin

  servings – amounts of food

Index

Copyright © 2003 by Robin Nelson

All rights reserved. International copyright secured. No part of this book may be reproduced, stored in a retrieval system, or transmitted in any form or by any means—electronic, mechanical, photocopying, recording, or otherwise—without the prior written permission of Lerner Publications Company, except for the inclusion of brief quotations in an acknowledged review.

The photographs in this books are reproduced through the courtesy of: © Todd Strand/ Independent Picture Service, front cover, pp. 3, 4, 5, 13, 15, 16, 22 (top, second from bottom, bottom); © PhotoDisc/Royalty-Free, pp. 2, 6, 8, 9, 11, 12, 22 (second from top, middle); © Corbis Royalty-Free Images, pp. 7, 14; © USDA/Ken Hammond, p. 10; © Rubberball Productions, p. 17.

Illustration on page 18 by Bill Hauser.

Lerner Publications Company
A division of Lerner Publishing Group
241 First Avenue North
Minneapolis, MN 55401 USA

Website address: www.lernerbooks.com

Library of Congress Cataloging-in-Publication Data

Nelson, Robin, 1971–
    Meats and proteins / by Robin Nelson.
       p.   cm. — (First step nonfiction)
    Includes index.
    ISBN: 0–8225–4630–2 (lib. bdg. : alk. paper)
    1. Meat—Juvenile literature. 2. Proteins in human nutrition—Juvenile literature. I. Title.
II. Series.
    TX373 .N45 2003
    613.2'82—dc21
                                                  2002013616

Manufactured in the United States of America
1 2 3 4 5 6 – JR – 08 07 06 05 04 03

Growing Readers
New Hanover County
Public Library
201 Chestnut Street
Wilmington, NC 28401